Pain Pushed Me Into My Purpose

VOL. 2

WALKED THROUGH THE FIRE BUT NOT BURNED

A poetry memoir by

SHAKIRA MCGEE

Copyright 2022

All rights reserved. This book or any portion thereof may not be reproduced or used in any manner whatsoever without the express written permission of the publisher except for the use of brief quotations in a book review.

ISBN: 978-1-66788-345-8

Preface

This book was inspired by the awe-inspiring God. This is a letter written to him that gives some background and insight into my story.

"Letter to My First Love"

I would like to thank you, God, for leading me to the scripture of Hosea chapters 1 & 2. Where you commanded Hosea to marry Gomer a prostitute who was an adulterous wife that rejected him. It was to illustrate to Israel how although you were her husband she was unfaithful to you, rejected you, didn't acknowledge you, forgot about you, and chased after idols and lovers. Blessing them with the blessings you gave her and giving them the credit for them. Lord, please forgive me because just like Israel I'm guilty of all these things too towards you. This scripture explains everything. I now understand why I've had to endure the pain of rejection all my life and never felt loved.

It's because I needed to experience the same pain we as sinners saved by grace have put you through but most of all so that you can get the glory out of it. Thank you for the lesson I got out of this and that's to still love others even when I don't feel so loved. Just like you do us. Thank you, God, for exposing my sins, judging me, and punishing me, alluring me, leading me into the wilderness, speaking to me tenderly, giving me a door of hope, accepting me back as your wife forever. Restoring our relationship, showing me unfailing love and compassion. Thank you for your everlasting mercy and Grace. Thank you for being my husband; in righteousness, justice, and faithfulness. Making me yours and declaring that I will know and acknowledge you.

Introduction

DON'T BE AFRAID TO WALK ALONE

When Jesus had called the Twelve disciples together, he gave them power and authority to drive out all demons and to cure diseases, and he sent them out to proclaim the kingdom of God and to heal the sick. "Take nothing for your journey," he instructed them. "Don't take a walking stick, traveler's bag, food, money, or even a change of clothes. Whatever house you enter, stay there until you leave that town. If people do not welcome you, leave their town and shake the dust off your feet as a testimony against them." So, they set out and went from village to village, proclaiming the good news and healing people everywhere. **Luke 9:1-6**

He said to another man, "Follow me."

But he replied, "Lord, first let me go and bury my father."

Jesus said to him, "Let the dead bury their own dead, but you go and proclaim the kingdom of God."

Still another said, "I will follow you, Lord; but first let me go back and say goodbye to my family."

Jesus replied, "No one who puts a hand to the plow and looks back is fit for service in the kingdom of God." **Luke 9:59-62**

When God Is Your Best-friend Your Never Alone

Table of Contents

PREFACE
1

INTRODUCTION
3

FEAR OF REJECTION
9

DON'T BE AFRAID TO TRUST GOD & COMPLETELY LET GO
23

ABANDONMENT ISSUES
54

BOUNDARIES
73

BALANCE
89

VIGILANT
97

SELF-DISCIPLINE
103

COMPLACENT
114

FAMILY
122

ACCEPTED
128

I SAY YES TO THE CALL LORD
140

EPILOGUE
148

AUTHOR BIO
151

Pain Pushed Me Into My Purpose

VOL. 2

WALKED THROUGH THE FIRE BUT NOT BURNED

Fear Of Rejection

Just when I thought it was safe
and I was finally
moving forward.

I was met with the reason
I never liked being alone
and that was the fear of rejection;
I instantly had to stop
and pull over.

She reminded me of how
I never felt loved,
understood,
valued,
appreciated,
my feelings validated,
good enough,
nor accepted
for who I truly am
by anyone.

Which caused all kinds of
pain, fears, and mixed emotions.

This time sadly I had
nowhere to hide or run.

I couldn't help but to
tune in, listen,
and try to stay focused.

Being a people pleaser,
too available,
seeking the approval of others,
caring about what other people think
and trying to fit in;
all fit the description.

This made me evaluate my life,
do some deep reflecting,
and soul searching.

It's time that I reframe
my way of thinking.

Lord knows I was tired
of my heart hurting.

For so long I settled
for the bare minimum
allowing people to dim my light and
walk all over me
like a doormat
because I didn't want to face
the fear of rejection
and being alone.

I was so caught up
in trying to please them,
showing my love,
and proving my loyalty;
yet losing myself.

Knowing deep down inside
I wasn't happy
and my house
was not a home.

FEAR NOT, FOR I AM WITH YOU. I AM YOUR GOD. I WILL strengthen YOU. I WILL help YOU. I WILL UPHOLD YOU WITH MY righteous RIGHT HAND.

ISAIAH 41:10

Don't Be Afraid To Trust God & Completely Let Go

Still holding on to
the memories,
the deceit,
the hurt,
the betrayal,
the pain.

I learned
I had to let it all go
completely.

The pictures,
the videos,
the
thoughts.

The delusion
that had my mind
and heart so caught.

and all the ways that wickedness deceives those who are perishing. They perish because they refused to love the truth and so be saved. For this reason, God sends them a powerful delusion so that they will believe the lie.

2 Thessalonians 2:10

See the pain
of my last relationship
opened up a deep old wound
that needed to be healed.

It nearly destroyed,
drained,
and sucked
the life out of me.

Until I had
nothing else
to give.

I was thinking
we would be together forever;
for better or worse, for richer or poorer, in
sickness and in health, to love and to cherish,
till death do us part.

Sadly,
that wasn't
the case.

It ended in divorce
we were unequally yoked;
failure from the start.

> DO NOT BE UNEQUALLY YOKED TOGETHER WITH UNBELIEVERS. FOR WHAT FELLOWSHIP HAS RIGHTEOUSNESS WITH LAWLESSNESS? AND WHAT COMMUNION HAS LIGHT WITH DARKNESS?
>
> **2 CORINTHIANS 6:14**

It was toxic;
I was sleep
nose wide open
blinded by lust.

The bad
outweighed
the good.

> **DO NOT BE DECEIVED BAD COMPANY CORRUPTS GOOD CHARACTER.**
>
> **1 CORINTHIANS 15:33**

**Absolutely
no trust!**

It truly took a toll on me;
broke my heart.

I stayed attached
stuck for so many years
because of a stronghold
that just wouldn't
let me depart.

FOR THOUGH WE WALK IN THE FLESH WE DO NOT WAR AFTER THE FLESH. FOR THE WEAPONS OF OUR WARFARE ARE NOT CARNAL, BUT MIGHTY THROUGH GOD TO THE PULLING DOWN OF STRONG HOLDS. CASTING DOWN IMAGINATIONS AND EVERY HIGH THING THAT EXALTED ITSELF AGAINST THE KNOWLEDGE OF GOD AND BRINGING INTO CAPTIVITY EVERY THOUGHT TO THE OBEDIENCE OF CHRIST.

        2 CORINTHIANS 10:3-5 KJV

I had gotten
comfortable
it was all
I knew.

By the Grace of God
one day I had
a spiritual awakening,
decided to rise up,
and knew
I had to choose.

Me that is;
Through prayer,
fasting,
stepping out on faith,
and taking action.

THEN CAME THE DISCIPLES TO JESUS PRIVITELY AND SAID. WHY COULD NOT WE CAST HIM OUT? AND JESUS SAID UNTO THEM, BECAUSE OF YOUR UNBELIEF: FOR VERILY I SAY UNTO YOU, IF YE HAVE FAITH AS A GRAIN OF MUSTARD SEED, YE SHALL SAY UNTO THIS MOUNTAIN, REMOVE HENCE TO YONDER PLACE; AND IT SHALL REMOVE; AND NOTHING SHALL BE IMPOSSIBLE UNTO YOU. HOWBELT THIS KIND GOETH NOT OUT BUT BY PRAYER AND FASTING.

MATTHEW 17:19-21 KJV

I was in it
for all those years
for love.

But, it would hurt me more
holding on to what was not meant
and blocking what God
was trying to send me
from above.

It's true when they say
people are in your life
for a season,
reason,
or a lifetime.

In my case
it's up to you
to get the lesson
before it's too late
and get out
trusting the process.

Moving on
embracing your journey;
believing that everything
is going to work out
just fine.

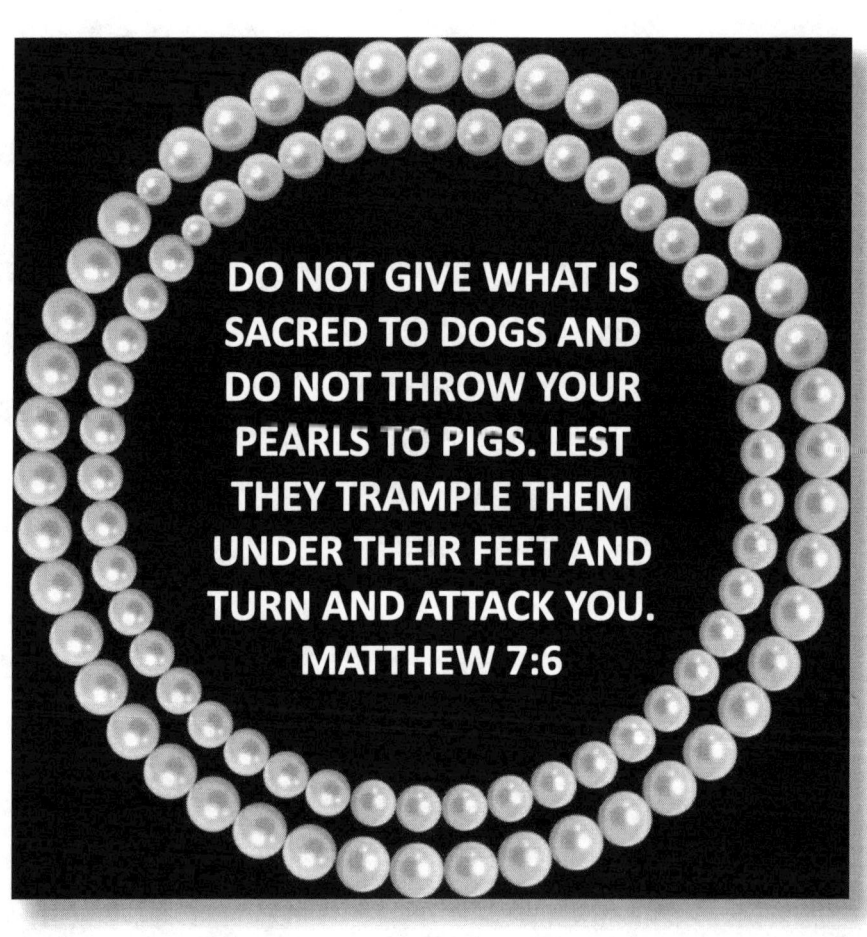

> Therefore, hear this, you afflicted one,
> made drunk, but not with wine. This is what your
> Sovereign Lord says,
> your God, who defends his people:
> "See, I have taken out of your hand
> the cup that made you stagger;
> from that cup, the goblet of my wrath,
> you will never drink again.
> I will put it into the hands of your tormentors,
> who said to you,
> 'Fall prostrate that we may walk on you.'
> And you made your back like the ground,
> like a street to be walked on."
>
> **Isaiah 51:21-23**

Abandonment Issues

That is where I found
abandonment issues
while digging up my pain
to the root.

Being half raised
by my grandmother
and being left
for months at a time
throughout the years
while my mother
was gone.

Made me always feel
second to best
because my grandmother already
had kids
younger than me
to raise on her own.

My grandmother
tried the best she could
but replacing my mother
was just something
she couldn't do.

Which, as a child
often left me feeling
lost
and somewhat confused.

I learned
different coping mechanisms
to deal
with the pain.

Running from it
was number one
to protect my heart
and keep my mind
from going insane.

There were times
when I felt
inadequate
and incomplete;
like a void
inside of me
that needed
to be filled.

Missing the love of a mother;
My mother.

So, for years
I chased
after it in others;
like I was seeking
my last meal.

Only to not find it
and be hurt
over and over again.

It became my new normal;
life
was like a big game.

That I
so desperately
needed to change.

I had to let go of the bitterness,
unforgiveness,
and resentment
that I held in my heart
towards my mother
for all those years.

Realizing
and accepting
that she did
the best she could
with what
she had to give.

On the day you were born your cord was not cut, nor were you washed with water to make you clean, nor were you rubbed with salt or wrapped in cloths. No one looked on you with pity or had compassion enough to do any of these things for you. Rather, you were thrown out into the open field, for on the day you were born you were despised.

"'Then I passed by and saw you kicking about in your blood, and as you lay there in your blood I said to you, "Live!" I made you grow like a plant of the field. You grew and developed and entered puberty. Your breasts had formed and your hair had grown, yet you were stark naked.

"'Later I passed by, and when I looked at you and saw that you were old enough for love, I spread the corner of my garment over you and covered your naked body. I gave you my solemn oath and entered into a covenant with you, declares the Sovereign Lord, and you became mine.

"'I bathed you with water and washed the blood from you and put ointments on you. I clothed you with an embroidered dress and put sandals of fine leather on you. I dressed you in fine linen and covered you with costly garments. I adorned you with jewelry: I put bracelets on your arms and a necklace around your neck, **and** I put a ring on your nose, earrings on your ears and a beautiful crown on your head. So, you were adorned with gold and silver; your clothes were of fine linen and costly fabric and embroidered cloth. Your food was honey, olive oil and the finest flour. You became very beautiful and rose to be a queen. And your fame spread among the nations on account of your beauty, because the splendor I had given you made your beauty perfect, declares the Sovereign Lord.

Ezekiel 16:4-14

(Tears) Lord, I thank you so much for leading me to this scripture years ago acknowledging that you know exactly what I've had to endure since a child. Thank you for reminding me and showing me that you were always there. Thank you for understanding me and being that voice when I couldn't speak. Thank you for showing me love and compassion when no one else did. Thank you for seeing me and crowning me as your beautiful queen.

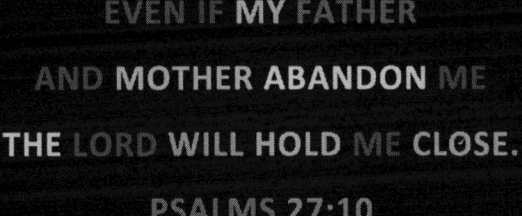

> EVEN IF **MY** FATHER
> AND **MOTHER ABANDON** ME
> **THE** LORD **WILL HOLD** ME **CLOSE.**
> PSALMS 27:10

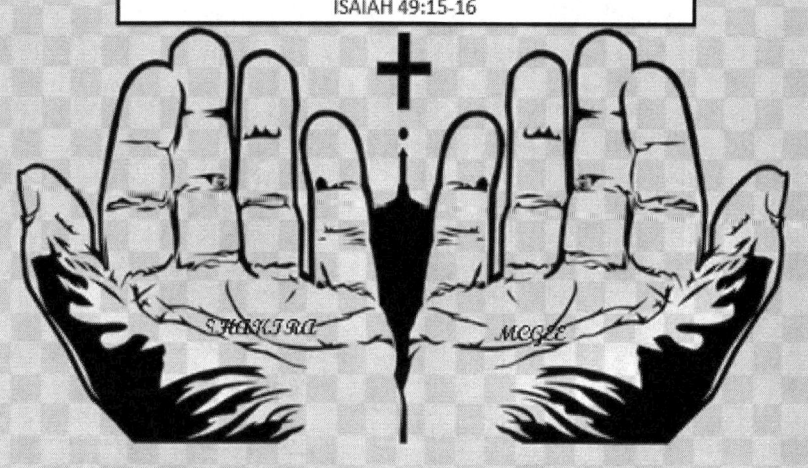

Boundaries

Tired of being hurt
and trying
to numb the pain.

Is when I ran
into boundaries
and things slowly
started to change.

They gave me
a sense of strength
that I needed
to face reality.

That overindulging
myself into people
was not
going to make them
change
or love me.

It was becoming
too much
so, I started setting limits,
saying no,
and eventually
I backed up
from it all.

So, that I could see
and think clearly
without having
to build a wall.

My vision
became clearer
and I got
to see me.

It was within
the triggers
that was not
setting me
all the way free.

I was more focused
on the actions
of other people.

Instead of seeking
the lesson
that God
was trying
to teach me.

Which was
that he allowed
everyone to reject me
for a reason.

So, the pain
could push me
into my
appointed season.

A season of
not being afraid
to walk alone.

Where he was
taking me.

All I needed
was him
the one who
sits high
on the throne.

Balance

I could not
move forward
in life
without balance.

I needed him
like an act
needs talent.

Balance taught me
to not bite
off more
then I can chew.

Letting go
of some people,
places,
and things
is something
I had to do.

I had to learn
to show up for myself,
before I could ever
show up for anything
or anyone else.

That's when
the peace
started relieving
the stress.

My days of feeling
overwhelmed
became days of feeling
pure blessed.

> **Deuteronomy 25:13-16 NIV**
>
> Do not have two differing weights in your bag—one heavy, one light. Do not have two differing measures in your house—one large, one small. You must have accurate and honest weights and measures, so that you may live long in the land the LORD your God is giving you. For the LORD your God detests anyone who does these things, anyone who deals dishonestly.

Vigilant

Being taken
advantage of;
made me realize
how blind
and naive I was.

Although, I had
forgiven everyone else.
I realized
for allowing
what happened to me;
I needed
to forgive myself.

Thank you,
God,
for sending vigilant
because she taught me
how to be harmless
as a dove
yet wise
as a serpent.

Now I'm watchful
and careful
with the choices
and decisions
that I make.

One mistake
can cause you
your whole life
and that's too big
of a risk
that I'm willing
to take.

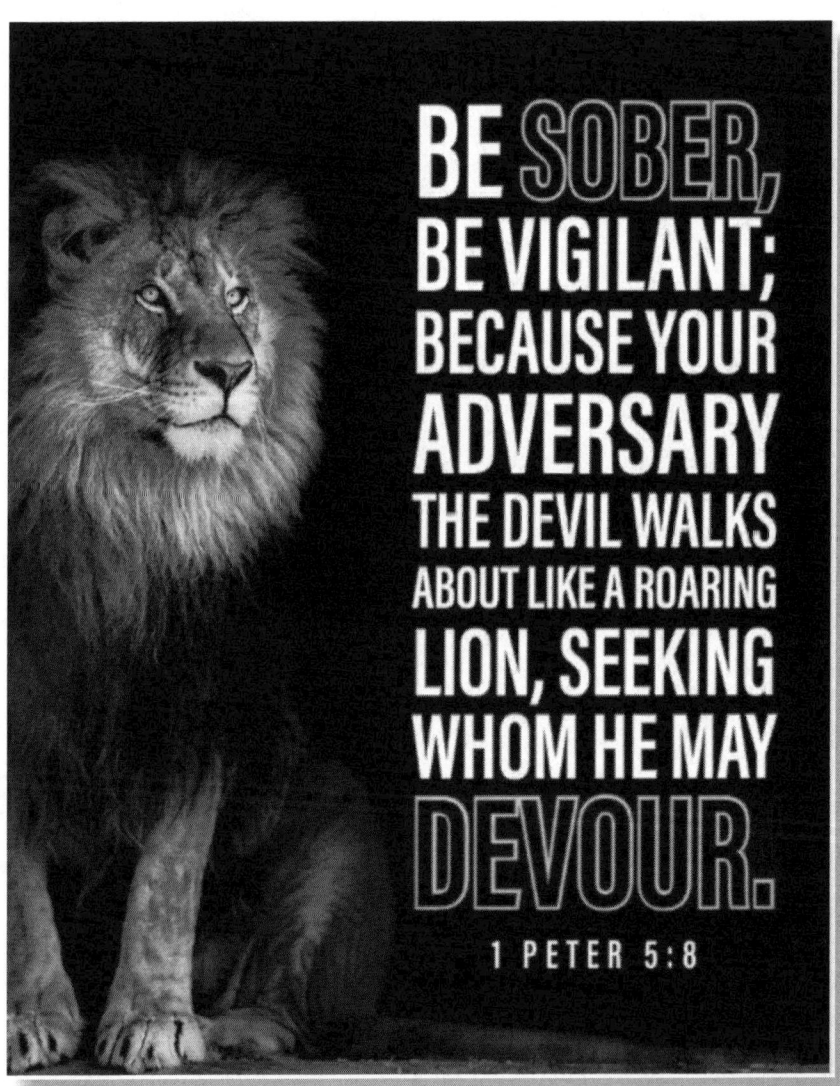

Self-Discipline

I came across self-discipline
and I knew I needed her
and that she was important
because my life
was spiraling
out of control.

So many ups
and downs
bringing me back
to the same place.

Like a revolving circle;
taking it all in
was hard to unfold.

She showed me how
I was burning myself out
and told me
that I can't just do
what I want to do
because I'm grown.

If I wanted to finish this race;
I needed to know
the race
is not given
to the swift
nor battle
to the strong.

I have to endure
to the end
by denying my flesh,
listening,
and doing
what's pleasing
to the Spirit.

So, that I can persevere
and overcome
my weaknesses.

Seeing real change,
results,
and even feel it.

She was a big
eye opener for me.

That I definitely needed
to hear and see.

SELF-DISCIPLINE

DOING WHAT YOU KNOW NEEDS TO BE DONE EVEN WHEN YOU DON'T FEEL LIKE IT....

Complacent

I reached complacent
when I thought
that I had arrived
and my spot was secure.

God put a deep sorrow
in my spirit
to warn me
nobody's coast is clear.

**I got the
message quick.**

To humble myself
and never get too comfortable
with my place of status
because I can be brought down
just as fast as I was lifted up
without a leave of absence.

I had to get outside
of myself
so that I
could make a difference
to others.

Striving to be a better me
each
and every day.

By being kind
and showing genuine love
towards my sisters
and brothers.

Amos 6:1

Woe to you who are complacent in Zion, and to you who feel secure on Mount Samaria, you notable men of the foremost nation, to whom the people of Israel come!

Family

While facing the pain
of my reality.

I learned the true
meaning of family.

I always thought that family
were the ones
related to you by blood.

Little did I know
I would soon find out
those people are just your relatives
and your real family
are the ones
who does the will of God
from above.

> **DON'T TRUST ANYONE- NOT YOUR BEST FRIEND OR EVEN YOUR WIFE! FOR THE SON DESPISES HIS FATHER. THE DAUGHTER DEFIES HER MOTHER. THE DAUGHTER –IN– LAW DEFIES HER MOTHER-IN-LAW. YOUR ENEMIES ARE RIGHT IN YOUR OWN HOUSEHOLD!**
>
> **MICAH 7:5-6**

> **Mark 3:31-35**
>
> Then Jesus' mother and brothers arrived. Standing outside, they sent someone in to call him. A crowd was sitting around him, and they told him, "Your mother and brothers are outside looking for you." "Who are my mother and my brothers?" he asked. Then he looked at those seated in a circle around him and said, "Here are my mother and my brothers! Whoever does God's will is my brother and sister and mother."

FAMILY

Accepted

I was embraced
with acceptance by God
showing me that
I didn't have to try to fit in;
I'm a natural- born leader
who was made to stand out.

Learning to embrace
my calling
no matter
how many times
my mind
tried to convince me
to have doubts.

Even Jesus
was not recognized
and rejected
by his own people.

The ones closest to you
can be
the most deceitful.

My spirit was telling me
that despite it all
I needed to keep
shining bright.

No longer being distracted
by the things of this world
and to continue walking
into my God- given light.

I maybe rejected by man
and not honored
in my own hometown.

> Then Jesus told them,
>
> "A prophet is honored everywhere except in his own hometown and among his relatives and his own family"
>
> **Mark 6:4**

But, I'm chosen by God
for great honor
along with the one
who laid down his life for me
on the cross
and borne the pain
of a thorn crown.

No more ignoring the signs
and the voice of God;
hurting myself
trying to force
different relationships.

Now I'm only showing up
where I'm celebrated,
appreciated,
and the energy is reciprocated
not just tolerated.

I Say Yes To The Call Lord

Just when I thought
I was getting closer
to the finish line
and everything
was working out
just fine.

Here come the triggers
showing me
that I have areas
that are still not healed.

If they were
I wouldn't be letting
the actions of other people
have that much power over me;
to determine how I feel.

It was like a slap in the face
after all of the hard work
I'd put in.

I went through moments
of anger,
frustration,
and times I didn't
even understand.

I had to realize
no matter
what I do or did.

I can't do it by myself
I need God;
in order for my ending
to be better than it began.

> I AM THE VINE; YOU ARE THE BRANCHES. IF YOU REMAIN IN ME AND I IN YOU, YOU WILL BEAR MUCH FRUIT: APART FROM ME YOU CAN DO NOTHING.
>
> JOHN 15:5

Epilogue

"Arise, shine, for your light has come,
and the glory of the Lord rises upon you.
See, darkness covers the earth
and thick darkness is over the peoples,
but the Lord rises upon you
and his glory appears over you
Nations will come to your light,
and kings to the brightness of your dawn.
"Lift up your eyes and look about you:
All assemble and come to you;
your sons come from afar,
and your daughters are carried on the hip.
Then you will look and be radiant,
your heart will throb and swell with joy;
the wealth on the seas will be brought to you,
to you the riches of the nations will come.
Herds of camels will cover your land,
young camels of Midian and Ephah.
And all from Sheba will come,
bearing gold and incense
and proclaiming the praise of the Lord.
All Kedar's flocks will be gathered to you,
the rams of Nebaioth will serve you;
they will be accepted as offerings on my altar,
and I will adorn my glorious temple.
"Who are these that fly along like clouds,
like doves to their nests?

Surely the islands look to me;
in the lead are the ships of Tarshish,
bringing your children from afar,
with their silver and gold,
to the honor of the Lord your God,
the Holy One of Israel,
for he has endowed you with splendor.
"Foreigners will rebuild your walls,
and their kings will serve you.
Though in anger I struck you,
in favor I will show you compassion.
Your gates will always stand open,
they will never be shut, day or night,
so that people may bring you the wealth of the nations their kings led in
triumphal procession.
For the nation or kingdom that will not serve you will perish;
it will be utterly ruined.
"The glory of Lebanon will come to you,
the juniper, the fir and the cypress together,
to adorn my sanctuary;
and I will glorify the place for my feet.
The children of your oppressors will come bowing before you;
all who despise you will bow down at your feet
and will call you the City of the Lord,
Zion of the Holy One of Israel.
"Although you have been forsaken and hated,
with no one traveling through,
I will make you the everlasting pride
and the joy of all generations.
You will drink the milk of nations
and be nursed at royal breasts.

Then you will know that I, the Lord, am your Savior,
your Redeemer, the Mighty One of Jacob.
Instead of bronze I will bring you gold,
and silver in place of iron.
Instead of wood I will bring you bronze,
and iron in place of stones.
I will make peace be your governor
and well-being your ruler.
No longer will violence be heard in your land,
nor ruin or destruction within your borders,
but you will call your walls Salvation
and your gates Praise.
The sun will no more be your light by day,
nor will the brightness of the moon shine on you,
for the Lord will be your everlasting light,
and your God will be your glory.
Your sun will never set again,
and your moon will wane no more;
the Lord will be your everlasting light,
and your days of sorrow will end.
Then all your people will be righteous
and they will possess the land forever.
They are the shoot I have planted,
the work of my hands,
for the display of my splendor.
The least of you will become a thousand,
the smallest a mighty nation.
I am the Lord;

in its time I will do this swiftly."

Isaiah 60:1-22

Author Bio

Shakira is a Daughter of the Most High
one and only God.
She is thankful to him
for blessing her
with a healing gift
of writing poetry.
Releasing her
from the bondage
of her past.
Giving her
a safe space
to speak her truth.
Allowing her
to say more in this book.
Freeing
and giving
that broken little girl
inside of her
a voice
to finally
be heard.